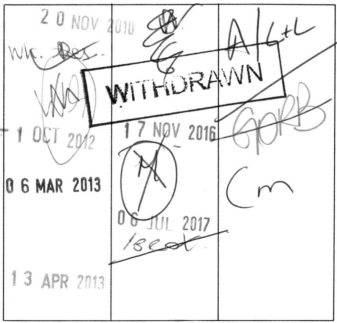

HOLIDAYS AND FESTIVALS

Chinese New Year

Nancy Dickmann

www.raintreepublishers.co.uk
Visit our website to find out
more information about
Raintree books.

To order:
☎ Phone 0845 6044371
🖷 Fax +44 (0) 1865 312263
🖳 Email myorders@raintreepublishers.co.uk

Customers from outside the UK please telephone +44 1865 312262

Raintree is an imprint of Capstone Global Library Limited, a company
incorporated in England and Wales having its registered office at 7 Pilgrim
Street, London, EC4V 6LB – Registered company number: 6695582

Text © Capstone Global Library Limited 2011
First published in hardback in 2011
The moral rights of the proprietor have been asserted.

Edited by Sian Smith, Nancy Dickmann, and Rebecca Rissman
Designed by Steve Mead
Picture research by Elizabeth Alexander
Production by Victoria Fitzgerald
Originated by Capstone Global Library Ltd
Printed and bound in China by South China Printing Company Ltd

ISBN 978 0 431 00686 4
14 13 12 11 10
10 9 8 7 6 5 4 3 2 1

British Library Cataloguing in Publication Data
Dickmann, Nancy.
   Chinese New Year. -- (Holidays and festivals)
   1. Chinese New Year--Pictorial works--Juvenile
literature.
   I. Title II. Series
   394.2'614'0951-dc22

Acknowledgements
We would like to thank the following for permission to reproduce
photographs: Alamy pp. **7** (© View Stock), **11** (© discpicture); Corbis pp.
4, **10** (© Ken Seet), **5** (© Yang Liu), **14** (© Redlink), **15** (© GARRIGE HO/
Reuters), **18** (© TIM CHONG/Reuters), **19** (© PRODPRAN JEERANGSAWAD/
epa), **23 top** (© PRODPRAN JEERANGSAWAD/epa); Getty Images pp. **8**
(JAY DIRECTO/AFP), **9** (Sean Justice/Riser), **16** (Asia Images Group), **17** (blue
jean images), **20** (ChinaFotoPress); Photolibrary pp. **6** (Blue Jean Images
LLC), **12** (Jack Hollingsworth/Asia Images), **13** (Panorama Media), **21**, **23**
middle (Elan Fleisher/LOOK-foto), **23 bottom** (Jack Hollingsworth/Asia
Images); shutterstock p. **22** (© Chunni4691).

Front cover photograph of decorative Chinese dragon reproduced with
permission of Getty Images (DAJ). Back cover photograph reproduced with
permission of Corbis (© TIM CHONG/Reuters).

We would like to thank Diana Bentley, Dee Reid, Nancy Harris, and
Richard Aubrey for their invaluable help in the preparation of this book.

Every effort has been made to contact copyright holders of material
reproduced in this book. Any omissions will be rectified in subsequent
printings if notice is given to the publishers.

Contents

What is a festival?

A festival is a time when people come together to celebrate.

Chinese people celebrate New Year in January or February.

People say goodbye to the old year.

They hope for good luck in the
new year.

Celebrating Chinese New Year

Chinese New Year celebrations last for fifteen days.

It is a time for visiting family.

People eat a special meal on
New Year's Eve.

People wear new clothes.

lion

People watch lion dances.

People give gifts.

People give red envelopes with money inside.

People watch fireworks.

Bringing good luck

People clean their houses for Chinese New Year.

They believe a clean house will bring good luck.

Red is a lucky colour in China.

banners

People hang red banners. The words bring good luck.

Lantern Festival

The last day of the festival is the
Lantern Festival.

lantern

Colourful lanterns light up the sky.

Things to look for

rat

ox

tiger

rabbit

dragon

snake

horse

goat

monkey

rooster

dog

pig

Have you seen these animals?
One is used to celebrate each
Chinese New Year.

22

Picture glossary

 **banner** piece of cloth or paper that can be hung as a decoration. Some banners have messages written on them.

 **lantern** holder for a candle or light. Some lanterns glow when they are lit.

 **lion dance** special dance that some Chinese people do. They pretend to be lions.

Index

Notes for parents and teachers

Before reading

Ask the children if they have ever celebrated New Year. Do they know when the new year begins? Make a list of different things they have done to celebrate New Year. Ask them if they can think of any other types of new year celebrations.

After reading

• Explain that some cultures use different calendars, so their new year celebrations do not always fall in January. The Chinese New Year is based on a lunar (moon) calendar, which is why it falls on a different date each year.

• Help the children to make their own Chinese New Year banners, using red paper for good luck. Show them some examples of Chinese calligraphy. Suggest that they spell out their names or messages of good luck.

• Explain that in the Chinese system, each year is associated with a particular animal. Information on this can be found at: www.topmarks.co.uk/chinesenewyear. Explain that some people think that people born under the same animal have similar characteristics, for example they could be wise or brave. Work with the children to brainstorm a list of characteristics that might be associated with the current year's animal.